Martin Leman

TEN CATS
and their Tales

HOLT, RINEHART AND WINSTON – NEW YORK

First published in the United States in 1982 by
Holt, Rinehart and Winston, 383 Madison Avenue,
New York, New York 10017.

Library of Congress Cataloging in Publication Data

Leman, Martin.
Ten cats and their tales.
Summary: Ten cats are shown engaging in ten
typically feline activities.
1. Counting—Juvenile literature.
[1. Counting. 2. Cats] I. Title.
QA113.L45 1982   513'.2[E]   82-6050
ISBN 0-03-062176-3   AACR2

First American Edition

Printed in Italy by A. Mondadori Editore - Verona
10 9 8 7 6 5 4 3 2 1

ISBN 0-03-062176-3

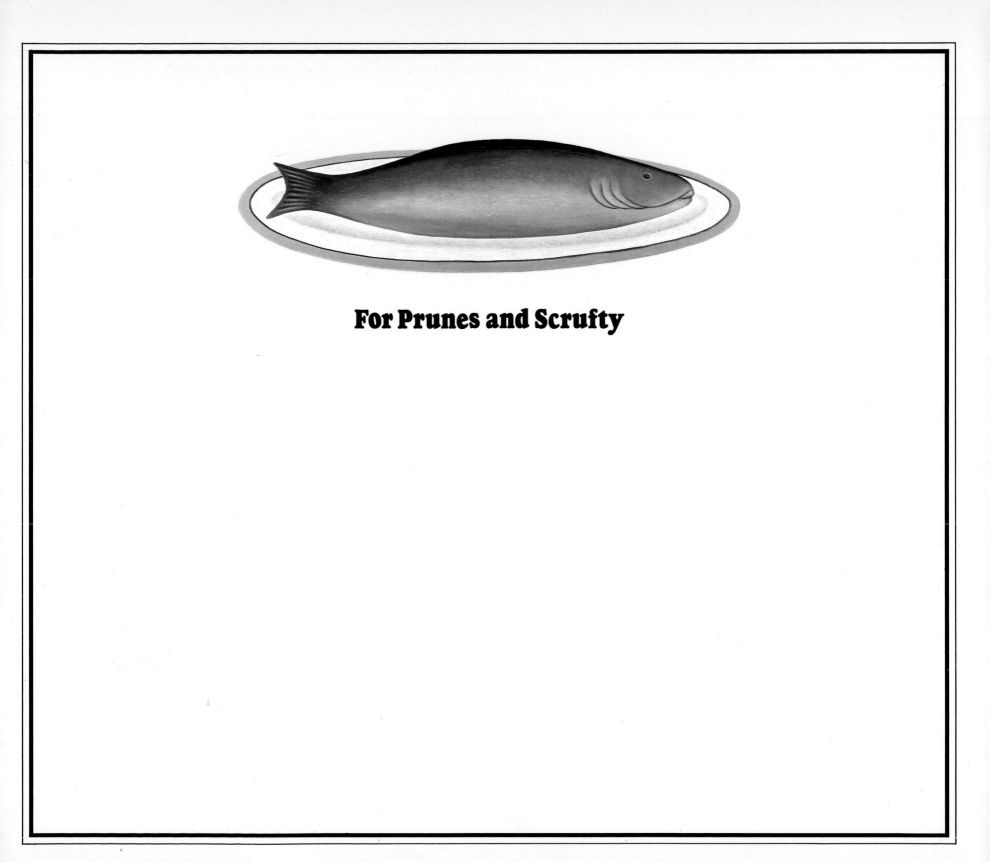

For Prunes and Scrufty

One is the cat
that sits on the mat

**Two is the cat
that grew very fat**

**Three is the cat
that lives by the sea**

**Four is the cat
that pounced on a bee**

**Five is the cat
that jumped on a wall**

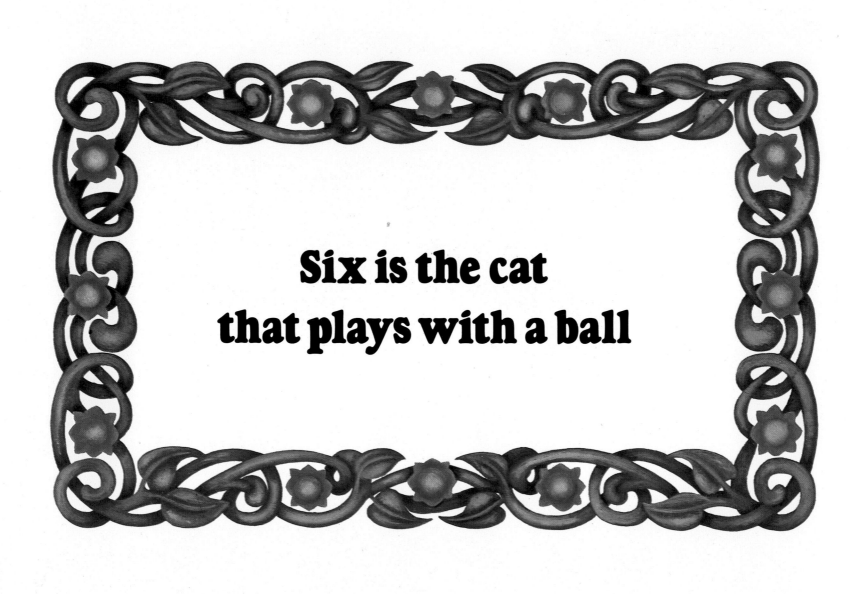

**Six is the cat
that plays with a ball**

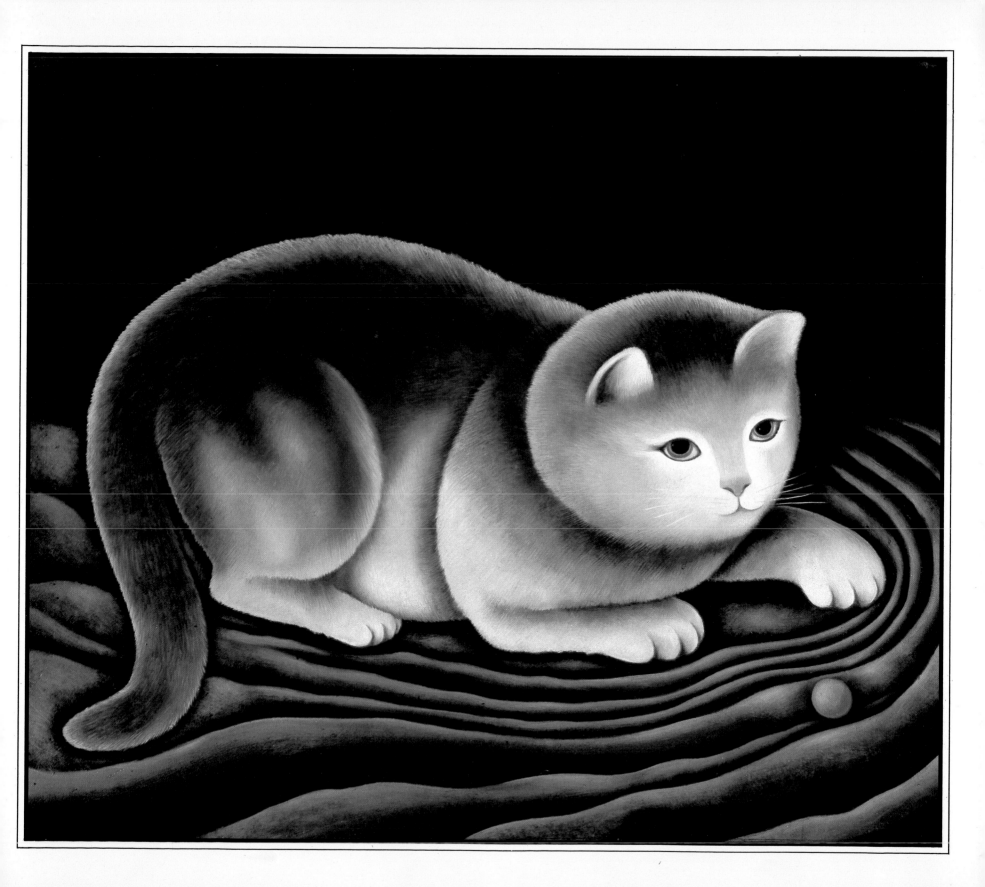

**Seven is the cat
that walks in the park**

**Eight is the cat
that can see in the dark**

Nine is the cat
whose best friend's a mouse

**Ten is the cat
that sleeps in the house**